History of America
Westward Expansion
1801 to 1850

Sally Senzell Isaacs

Heinemann LIBRARY

First published in Great Britain by Heinemann Library,
Halley Court, Jordan Hill, Oxford OX2 8EJ
a division of Reed Educational and Professional Publishing Ltd.
Heinemann is a registered trademark of Reed Educational & Professional Publishing Limited. Oxford, Melbourne, Auckland, Johannesburg, Blantyre, Gaborone, Ibadan, Portsmouth (NH) USA, Chicago

HISTORY OF AMERICA: WESTWARD EXPANSION
was produced for Heinemann Library
by Bender Richardson White.

Editor: Lionel Bender
Designer: Ben White
Assistant Editor: Michael March
Picture Researcher: Madeleine Samuel
Media Conversion and Typesetting: MW Graphics
Production Controller: Kim Richardson

03 02 01 00 99 98
10 9 8 7 6 5 4 3 2 1

Printed in Hong Kong

British Library Cataloguing-in-Publication Data.
Isaacs, Sally Senzell
  History of America : 1800 – 1850 Westward expansion
  1. United States - History - 19th century – Juvenile literature
  I. Title.
  973.5

ISBN 0431 05643 9 Hb   ISBN 0431 05648 X Pb

Special thanks to Mike Carpenter, Scott Westerfield and Tristan Boyer at Heinemann Library for editorial and design guidance and direction.

Any words appearing in the text in bold, **like this**, are explained in the Glossary.

Photo Credits:
Picture Research Consultants, Mass: pages 13 right (Anne S.K. Brown Military College), 14 (Slater Mill Historic Site), 26 (Library of Congress), 27 (Library of Congress), 31 (Courtesy of Samuel Herrup Antiques), 34 (Nebraska State Historical Society), 37 (Minnesota Historical Society), 38 (California State Library), 40 (T. W. Wood Gallery), 41 (Courtesy of the New York Historical Society, New York City). Peter Newark's American Pictures: pages 6, 8 right, 13 left, 15, 16, 18, 21, 23, 25, 28, 29, 30, 36, 39. North Wind Pictures: pages 8 left, 11, 19, 22, 33 top, 33 bottom, 35.

Every effort has been made to contact copyright holders of any material reproduced in this book. Omissions will be rectified in subsequent printings if notice is given to the publisher.

Artwork credits
Illustrations by: John James on pages 6/7, 8/9, 16/17, 28/29, 34/35; James Field on pages 12/13, 20/21, 24/25, 40/41; Mark Bergin on pages 10/11, 18/19, 26/27; Gerald Wood on pages 14/15, 22/23, 32/33, 38/39; Nick Hewetson on pages 30/31, 36/37. All maps by Stefan Chabluk.
Cover: Design and make-up by Pelican Graphics. Artwork by John James. Photos: Top: North Wind Pictures. Centre: Picture Research Consultants (Slater Mill Historic Site). Bottom: North Wind Pictures.

Major quotations used in this book come from the following sources. In some cases, quotes have been abridged for clarity:
Page 8: Jefferson's instructions to Lewis: *The Journals of Lewis and Clark*, edited by Bernard DeVoto. New York: Houghton Mifflin Company, 1953 and 1981, page 481.
Page 10: Clark's journal: *The Journals of Lewis and Clark*, edited by Bernard DeVoto, New York: Houghton Mifflin Company, 1953 and 1981, page 256.
Page 12: Madison's speech to Congress. *Documents of American History*, edited by Henry Steele Commager. New York: Appleton-Century Crofts, Inc., 1958, page 207.
Page 16: George Caitlin quote: *I Have Spoken—American History through the voices of the Indians*, compiled by Virginia Irving Armstrong. Chicago: Sage Books, The Swallow Press, Inc., 1971, page 69.
Page 18: Meeting between Osceola and General Thompson: From *Native American Testimony*. Edited by Peter Nabokov. New York: Thomas Y. Crowell, 1978, page 157.
Page 22: Diary of Susan Magoffin. From: *History of US* by Joy Hakim. New York: Oxford University Press, 1994, Book 5, page 26.
Page 36: James Polk's address to Congress: From *West of the West* by Robert Kirsch and William S. Murphy New York: E.P. Dutton & Co., Inc. 1967, pages 295-296.
Page 41. Immigrant quotes: *Our Country* (textbook). New York: Silver Burdett Ginn, 1995, page 404.

The Consultants

Special thanks to Diane Smolinski, Nancy Cope and Christopher Gibb for their help in the preparation of this book.

CONTENTS

History of America is a series of nine books arranged chronologically, meaning that events are described in the order in which they happened. However, since each book focuses on an important person in American history, the timespans of the titles overlap. In each book, most articles deal with a particular event or part of American history. Others deal with aspects of everyday life, such as trade, houses, clothing and farming. These general articles cover longer periods of time. The little illustrations at the top left of each article are a symbol of the times. They are identified on page 3.

▼ About the map
This map shows the United States today. It shows the boundaries and names of all the states. Refer to this map, or to the one on pages 42–43, to locate places talked about in this book.

About this book
This book is about America from 1801 to 1850. The terms America and US mean 'the United States of America'. By 1850, the 13 original colonies had grown into 31 united states. At first, all the western land was wilderness. Then borders were marked and the land became territories, such as Louisiana Territory and Ohio Territory. Once a territory had 60,000 free citizens, it could be admitted as a new state. We describe and illustrate the life histories of Lewis and Clark as the focal point of this expansion of America.

Some historians refer to the native people of America as Indians. Others call them Native Americans, as we do. Words in **bold** are described in more detail in the glossary on page 46.

INTRODUCTION

By the early 1800s, most Americans wanted their country to be as big as possible. Piece by piece, the United States government claimed or purchased land from the Atlantic to the Pacific Oceans.

Meriwether Lewis and William Clark were two brave men assigned to explore America's new land. In a daring expedition, joined by 30 to 40 other explorers, they walked, paddled and rode horses from St Louis (now in the state of Missouri) to the Pacific Ocean. They drew maps, took notes and made friends – and sometimes fought – with Native Americans. Thanks to the work of Lewis and Clark, later explorers and settlers had information about the land, animals, weather and people of the West.

Some pages in the book tell about the journey of Lewis and Clark. Those pages that describe other events in America include yellow boxes that tell you what Lewis and Clark were doing at the time. Lewis and Clark died before many of the events in this book took place. They never saw wagon trains crossing the Great Plains or mining towns in California. Still, their brave adventures gave other Americans the courage to go west!

As you read this book, use the map on pages 42 and 43 to follow the trails of Lewis and Clark and the Americans who followed them.

A NEW PRESIDENT

Thomas Jefferson was a new kind of American president. He did not ride in the presidential coach; he rode a horse. He placed his dinner guests at a round table so no one felt more or less important. He believed all citizens were equal. But he had slaves.

Every year, on New Year's Day and 4 July (Independence Day), Jefferson opened the President's House to all Americans who could get there. Rich and poor people were equally welcomed.

Jefferson was different from George Washington and John Adams. He thought the government should not interfere in people's lives. He cut taxes and reduced the size of the **military**. However, like the first two presidents, he worried about the other countries who owned land in North America.

Control of New Orleans

In 1802, the port of New Orleans in Louisiana belonged to France. Americans used this port to send their goods to markets. Farmers from places such as Illinois and Kentucky sent their crops down the Mississippi River to New Orleans, then into the Gulf of Mexico, and up the East Coast. Jefferson was afraid that France might one day stop Americans from using the port.

"Every eye in the United States is now fixed on the affairs of Louisiana", wrote President Jefferson in a letter to Robert Livingston, an American official living in France.

▲ This picture of Thomas Jefferson was painted by Rembrandt Peale in 1800. Thomas Jefferson was born in Virginia in 1743. His father was in Virginia's **House of Burgesses.**

Jefferson grew up on a **plantation**, or large farm, with at least 20 **slaves**. He went to college, became a lawyer and became very involved in colonial government. He married Martha Wayles Skelton and had six children.

The importance of Thomas Jefferson
Jefferson was known as a good lawyer and a good writer who used plain and simple English. This talent and his love of his country led to these important jobs in the United States:
• wrote the Declaration of Independence
• governor of Virginia
• US official in France
• US **secretary of state**
• vice-president of US
• US president. He became president in March 1801.

The Louisiana Purchase

In 1802, President Jefferson asked Robert Livingston to try to buy New Orleans from the French. He told Livingston to offer $10 million for the city. France's answer surprised them.

France offered to sell all of Louisiana for $15 million! France's ruler, Napoleon Bonaparte, was giving up on the idea of keeping colonies in America. He wanted money for the French army to fight his wars in Europe. Jefferson agreed to the deal. In October 1803, the US **Senate** approved. The United States doubled in size. No one asked the Native Americans who lived in Louisiana if they would agree to the deal.

◀ The Louisiana Purchase moved the **nation**'s western boundary from the Mississippi River to the Rocky Mountains. Later, this land would become these 13 states: Minnesota, Iowa, Missouri, Arkansas, Louisiana, Oklahoma, Kansas, Nebraska, South Dakota, North Dakota, Montana, Wyoming, Colorado.

◀ Flags are changed in New Orleans in 1803 to mark the Louisiana Purchase. At this ceremony, the French flag is taken down and the American 'Stars and Stripes' flag is raised.

LEWIS AND CLARK

Thomas Jefferson had hundreds of questions about his Louisiana Purchase. Was it a bargain or not? Was the land good for farming? Were the Native Americans friendly or warlike? Was there a way to cross the Rocky Mountains? Was there a major waterway to the Pacific Ocean?

Jefferson called in his private secretary, Meriwether Lewis. He knew that Lewis had served in the army on the **frontier.** He asked Lewis to consider leading a group of explorers through the rivers of the Louisiana **Territory**. Lewis wrote to his friend, William Clark, to ask him to join the group. Both men said yes.

Jefferson wrote instructions to Lewis. He wanted Lewis and Clark to bring back maps and written notes about: "the soil and face of the country...the animals of the country, generally, and especially those not known in the US...the mineral production of every kind...climate as characterized by...proportion of rainy, cloudy and clear days...the dates at which particular plants put forth or lose their flowers...times of appearance of particular birds, reptiles or insects."

Getting ready to go

Lewis and Clark were good partners because they were not alike. Lewis was shy and moody. He liked science and studying nature. Clark was cheerful and liked chatting with people. He was good at drawing maps.

Lewis and Clark spent months preparing for their trip. They:
• practised scientific methods for gathering seeds
• learned how to draw and identify animals
• studied Native American culture
• trained other men for the journey. Many of the group knew Native American languages.

▲ Lewis and Clark's largest boat was a keelboat like this one. It was 17 m long with a square sail and 22 oars for rowing.

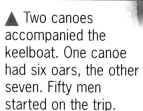

▲ Two canoes accompanied the keelboat. One canoe had six oars, the other seven. Fifty men started on the trip.

◀ Patrick Gass, a member of the expedition, drew this picture of a meeting with Sioux Native Americans in Iowa.

▲ When the explorers reached North Dakota in the winter of 1804, they met Sacagawea. She helped them communicate with Native Americans.

◀ By May 1805, the explorers have travelled the Missouri River to a narrowing in the Milk River (in present-day Montana). Lewis points out features of the land and water. Clark draws a map. A man named York is seated on the rock. He is Clark's **slave**. The team depends on his excellent hunting and fishing skills. Because of his dark skin, Native Americans trust him.

▲ The explorers had a well-equipped medicine chest with more than 20 remedies.

▲ As a symbol of friendship, Lewis and Clark gave Peace and Friendship Medals like these to Native American chiefs. The chiefs proudly wore the gifts on ribbons around their necks.

On 14 May 1804, Lewis and Clark's team of explorers gathered at the Missouri River near St Louis. They loaded these supplies onto their three boats: clothing, tools, guns, food and medical supplies. They also brought things to trade with the Native Americans: beads, ribbons, American flags, fish hooks and needles.

As the team started their journey, settlers from villages along the river cheered from the shore. Days later, they had left the villages behind. The explorers reached the quiet wilderness of unsettled territories.

DISCOVERIES

William Clark's journal, 19 October 1805: "I observed a great number of lodges on the opposite side [of the Columbia River]...and several Indians on the opposite bank....They returned to their lodges as fast as they could run. They said we...were not men."

Clark approached the lodge with trinkets and a peace pipe. The Native Americans were still frightened. Then Clark's Native American guide, Sacagawea, entered the lodge. Soon everyone relaxed and realized that the explorers were friendly. Lewis and Clark appreciated the help of the Native Americans they met. The Native Americans taught them where the rivers and waterfalls were and which animals and plants to eat.

Some highlights of the expedition

Spring 1804: They are hit by a violent tornado followed by "troublesome mosquitoes". *Summer 1804:* They observe pelicans, prairie dogs and buffalo. *Winter 1804:* They build a log fort outside a Mandan tribal village and wait for the bad weather to pass. *Spring 1805:* The Great Falls of the Missouri River is ahead. The explorers bury a canoe and some supplies. They build wooden carts to push their other canoes and supplies over land. The keelboat is sent back to St Louis.

▶ Lewis and Clark set out from St Louis on 14 May 1804. They travelled up the Missouri River in boats. Then they acquired horses from the Shoshone and crossed the Rocky Mountains. On 7 November 1805, they reached the Pacific Ocean. They built a winter camp, Fort Clastop. In the spring of 1806, they set off for home.

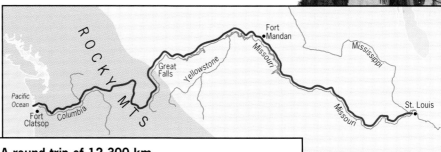

A round trip of 12,300 km

The team took 1 year, 5 months and 24 days to reach the Pacific Ocean. Eager to share their news and spending less time investigating, they made the return trip in just 6 months.

On their return journey, Lewis and Clark split up to try to find a shorter route over the Rocky Mountains. Lewis led a group directly east to the Missouri River. Clark almost retraced his steps, then followed the Yellowstone River to the Missouri River.

Lewis and Clark reunited in August 1806 and returned to St Louis.

GREAT PLAINS

- Spanish Territory
- Route
- River

0   250 miles
0   400 kilometres

◀ As the explorers crossed the **Great Plains**, they saw wild animals unfamiliar to them. They saw groups of prairie dogs (far left) that made their homes under the ground. They estimated that they saw 3000 buffalo.

▲ Lewis and Clark shoot a grizzly bear, an animal previously unknown to white people. This woodcut is by Patrick Gass of the expedition.

◀ On 17 August 1805, the explorers met with the Shoshone leader, Great Chief Chameahwait. The chief turned out to be Sacagawea's brother. The chief gave the explorers horses. He also gave advice about crossing the Rockies.

▼ This is what Clark's drawing of a sage grouse discovered by Lewis on 5 June 1805, looked like.

To the Pacific Ocean

Summer 1805: The river gets too shallow for canoes. They use horses to cross the Rocky Mountains. *Fall 1805:* On the far side of the Rockies, they build canoes and follow the Columbia River to the Pacific! *Spring 1806:* Start homeward.

Lewis and Clark collected a wealth of information about the newest part of the United States. For years after, settlers followed their trails.

THE WAR OF 1812

In 1806, when Lewis and Clark returned from the Pacific Ocean, France and Great Britain were at war again. The leader of France was trying to subdue Great Britain. Americans were suffering from this war even though they lived thousands of kilometres away.

American merchants had been trading with both Britain and France. Suddenly, both countries said they would capture any ships that traded with their enemy. American ships were captured by both sides. And Britain, more than France, forced American sailors to fight in its navy. Americans now resented the British.

The war of poor communications
Communications were very slow in the early 1800s. There was no telegraph and no telephone or radio. Messages were taken by horse, train or ship. On 16 June 1812, Britain promised to stop bothering American ships. The news did not reach America in time. On 18 June, US President James Madison asked **Congress** to declare war on Britain.

For over two years, America and Britain fought many battles in Canada. Finally, on 24 December 1814, **representatives** of the two countries signed a peace **treaty** in Ghent, Belgium. Again, news did not reach America in time. Fifteen days later, the war's bloodiest battle took place in New Orleans.

The War of 1812 was unusual in American history: it did not have a winner. Each country gave back the land it captured.

> **Lewis and Clark move on**
> In 1807, Meriwether Lewis became governor of the Louisiana Territory. He died in 1809. William Clark became governor of the Missouri Territory in 1813.

▼ America won its first battle on the waters of Lake Erie. On 10 September 1813, Commodore Oliver Perry's nine ships defeated Britain's six ships. Here, a British ship is being attacked. America won control of the lake and captured much of upper Canada.

> **Events in the war**
> **June 1812** US declares war on Great Britain
> **September 1813** US wins Battle of Lake Erie
> **August 1814** British burn the President's House (now called the White House) and Capitol in Washington, DC
> **December 1814** Treaty of Ghent ends War of 1812
> **January 1815** US wins Battle of New Orleans.
>
> **Meanwhile**
> In 1808, Congress passed a new law. **Slaves** could no longer be brought into the United States. But people could still buy slaves from other American slave-owners.

▲ Tecumseh was a Shawnee leader. He brought eastern Native Americans together to fight for their land. Tecumseh volunteered his people to help the British in the war. He was killed in battle by an American soldier on 5 October 1813, as shown in this 1840s **lithograph**.

▲ This **engraving** was made by an unknown artist in 1815 and is called Capture of City of Washington. The White House was only 14 years old when the British attacked Washington, DC and set the building on fire. Then they attacked Baltimore, in Maryland.

FACTORIES

In 1813, a Boston merchant named Francis Lowell visited England's cloth factories. He saw large machines making hundreds of yards of cotton cloth which were then shipped to America. "Why couldn't America make its own cloth?" he wondered.

New states and colonies of America
1803 Ohio statehood
1816 Indiana statehood
1817 Mississippi statehood
1818 Illinois statehood
1819 Alabama statehood
1819 US buys Florida from Spain
1820 Maine statehood
1821 Missouri statehood
1821 Stephen Austin starts an American colony in Mexico's Texas.

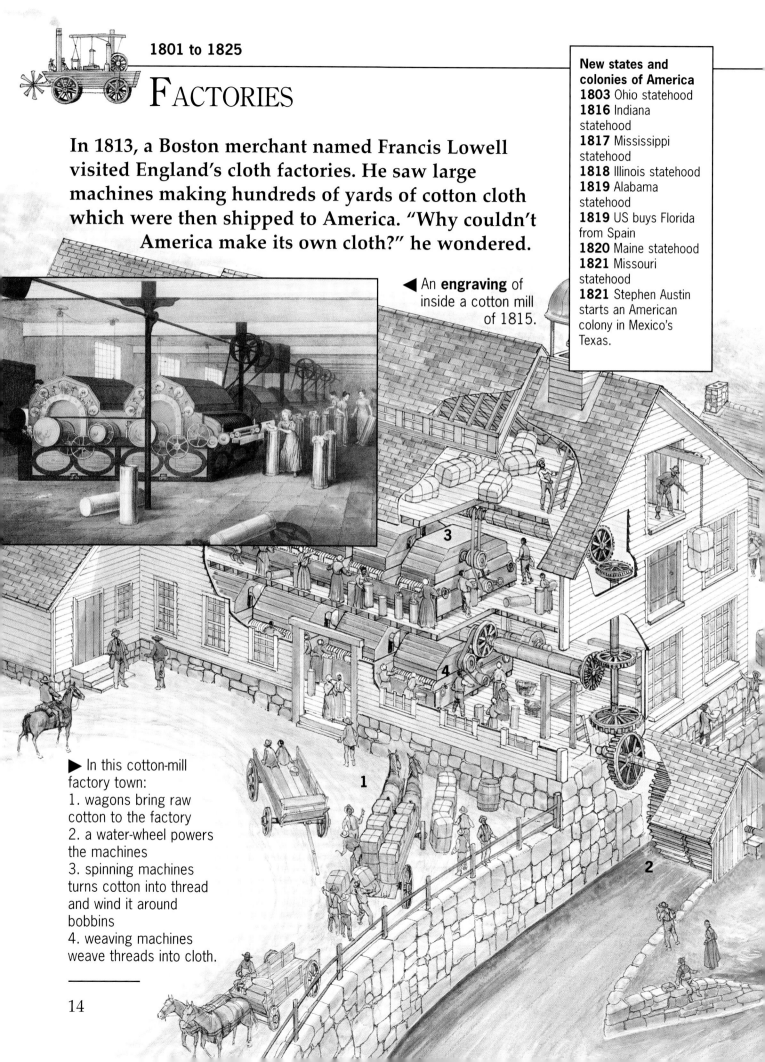

◀ An **engraving** of inside a cotton mill of 1815.

▶ In this cotton-mill factory town:
1. wagons bring raw cotton to the factory
2. a water-wheel powers the machines
3. spinning machines turns cotton into thread and wind it around bobbins
4. weaving machines weave threads into cloth.

14

Francis Lowell returned to America, and in 1814 built a cotton processing factory in Waltham, Massachusetts, not far from Boston. There were many machines in the factory. Some machines spun cotton into thread. Others wove the thread into cloth. The factory was built next to the Charles River. The rushing water powered a water-wheel, which powered the machines.

The first women factory workers

After Lowell's death in 1817, his business partners built a factory town, called Lowell, in Massachusetts. They built factories, shops, churches and **boarding-houses** for the employees. Many of the workers were teenage women from farms who had never been able to find full-time paid work before. They worked in the factories until they decided to marry.

▲ Lowell's factories processed raw cotton from **plantations** in the South. This **engraving** from 1800 shows a plantation-owner selling his cotton to a factory owner. Black **slaves** operate a cotton gin, which separated cotton fibres from the seeds.

▲ Children who worked in the factories were often told to get behind machines to fix broken threads. This was a dangerous job.

A changing world

Factory workers worked 12 hours a day, 6 days a week. Most workers were women and children. While parents stayed on their farms, sons and daughters worked in the factory towns. Cities grew around the factories. Then people started moving from farms to cities. This was the start of America's Industrial **Revolution**.

THE TRAIL OF TEARS

Clark's last years
William Clark was governor of Missouri Territory from 1813 to 1820. In 1808, he married Julia Hancock. She died in 1820 and he married Harriet Kennerly. They had five children. His three sons were named: Meriwether Lewis (after his partner), George Rogers (after his brother), and Jefferson (after the president). William Clark died in 1838.

In the 1820s, about 125,000 Native Americans lived east of the Mississippi River. They were the Creeks, Chickasaws, Cherokees, Choctaws and Seminoles. Many were happy to live among the white settlers. But the settlers were land-hungry. In 1835, US soldiers began forcing the Native Americans to leave their homes and walk 1400 km to land further west.

This long, sad journey has been called the Trail of Tears. George Catlin, an American artist during the 1830s, wrote about the Native Americans he saw: "I have seen him set fire to his wigwam and smooth over the graves of his fathers ...clap his hand in silence over his mouth, and take the last look over his fair hunting ground, and turn his face in sadness to the setting sun."

▶ In the winter of 1838-1839, more than 15,000 Native Americans marched west into unknown land, called 'Indian **Territory**' (which is today the state of Oklahoma). Along the trail, the Native Americans had little food and no shelter. At least 4000 of them died. This was called the Trail of Tears.

▶ In 1821, a Cherokee named Sequoyah completed 12 years of work on an alphabet of the Cherokee language. At last, the words of the great leaders could be written down and shared. People could communicate with each other by letters and newspapers.

Within a few years, almost all Cherokees learned to read. The *Cherokee Phoenix* was the Cherokee weekly newspaper. It was bilingual, written in both English and Cherokee. Sequoya's language was also used to write down the **constitution** of the Cherokee **Nation**. It was based on the United States Constitution.

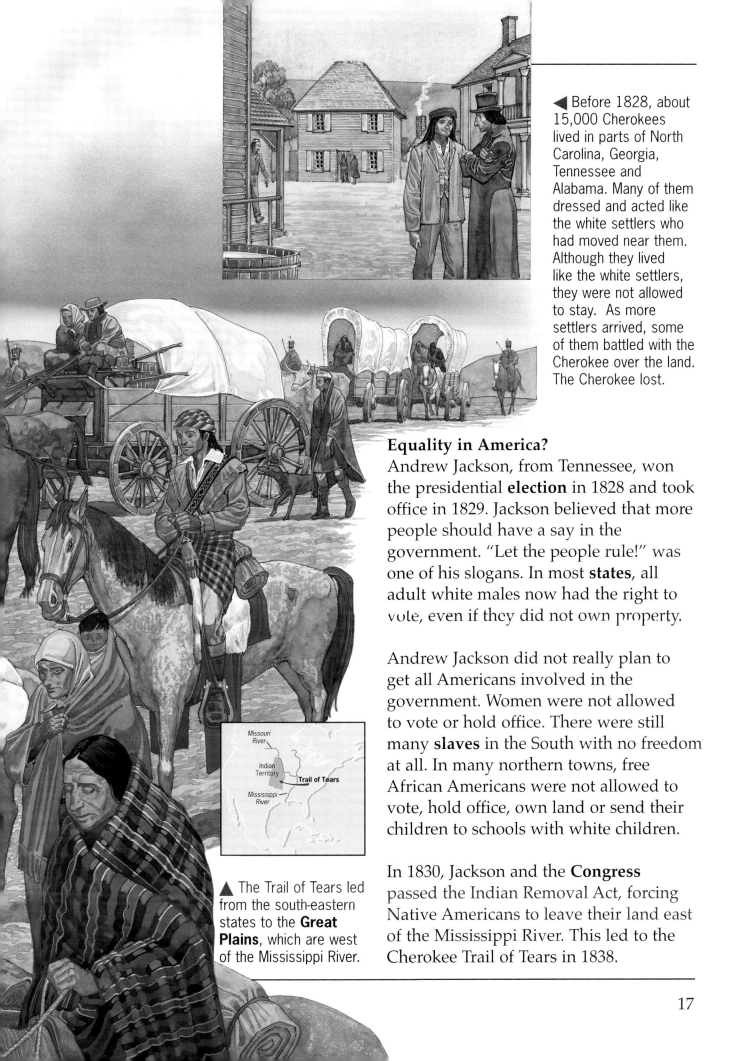

Before 1828, about 15,000 Cherokees lived in parts of North Carolina, Georgia, Tennessee and Alabama. Many of them dressed and acted like the white settlers who had moved near them. Although they lived like the white settlers, they were not allowed to stay. As more settlers arrived, some of them battled with the Cherokee over the land. The Cherokee lost.

The Trail of Tears led from the south-eastern states to the **Great Plains**, which are west of the Mississippi River.

Missouri River

Indian Territory

Trail of Tears

Mississippi River

Equality in America?

Andrew Jackson, from Tennessee, won the presidential **election** in 1828 and took office in 1829. Jackson believed that more people should have a say in the government. "Let the people rule!" was one of his slogans. In most **states**, all adult white males now had the right to vote, even if they did not own property.

Andrew Jackson did not really plan to get all Americans involved in the government. Women were not allowed to vote or hold office. There were still many **slaves** in the South with no freedom at all. In many northern towns, free African Americans were not allowed to vote, hold office, own land or send their children to schools with white children.

In 1830, Jackson and the **Congress** passed the Indian Removal Act, forcing Native Americans to leave their land east of the Mississippi River. This led to the Cherokee Trail of Tears in 1838.

THE US ARMY VS THE SEMINOLES

"Friends and Brothers: I come from your great father, the President of the United States....On the 9th of May, 1832, you entered into a treaty at Payne's Landing...you must prepare to move by the time the cold weather shall have passed away."

These were the words of US General Wiley Thompson at a meeting with some Seminole chiefs on 23 October 1834. From 1832 to 1834, the government had signed **treaties** with Seminole chiefs in Florida. The chiefs had agreed to leave the land. In exchange, they would get new land in Oklahoma, as well as cattle and money.

Yet many Seminoles refused to honour the treaty. Chief Osceola was one of them. He spoke up at this meeting with General Thompson: "My Brothers! The white people got some of our chiefs to sign a paper to give our lands to them, but our chiefs did not do as we told them to do. The agent tells us we must go away from the lands we live on – our homes, and the graves of our Fathers, and go over the big river [the Mississippi] among the bad Indians. When the agent tells me to go from my home, I hate him, because I love my home and will not go from it."

Three Seminole Wars
The Seminoles and the United States Army fought each other in:
1817–1818 The British, who claimed Florida, encouraged the Seminoles to fight American settlers.
1835–1842 The US Army forced Seminoles to move west.
1855–1858 Remaining Seminoles fought to stay on their land, then agreed to move west.

▶ The Seminoles prepare to **ambush** American soldiers who have arrived at one of Florida's swamplands. The Seminoles know the area well so they can hide among the swampy islands. The soldiers must wade through tall grasses just to find their enemy.

▲ At the same time, Cherokees who survived the Trail of Tears built log cabins like this one to live in.

▶ This picture of Seminole chief Osceola was painted by George Catlin in about 1835. In 1837, Osceola raised a white flag, asking for a truce. In the rules of war, when one side raises a white flag, both sides stop fighting and have a meeting. Instead, US General Thomas Jesup had his troops hidden around the meeting place. When Osceola arrived, he was captured. He died in jail of malaria in 1838.

St Augustine in Florida is the oldest permanent European settlement in the United States. It was founded by Spain in 1565. This woodcut shows a Spanish presidio (fort) during the days when Spain owned Florida. In 1821, Florida became a **territory** of the United States. Even today, St Augustine has many historic Spanish buildings.

A long, costly battle

In 1835, President Andrew Jackson sent the US army to Florida to move out the Seminoles. The Seminoles hid in the swamps, refusing to leave. Bitter fighting followed for the next seven years. Runaway **slaves** who were hiding in Florida helped the Seminoles fight. When the war ended in 1842, the United States had lost 1500 soldiers and $20 million. In 1835, there had been 5000 Seminoles living in Florida. By 1842, 400 had been killed, 4000 had moved to Indian Territory, and only 600 were left.

Both the US army and the Seminoles had guns and rifles. But the Seminoles had fewer weapons and fewer warriors. In addition, the Seminole leaders often could not agree on their battle plans.

19

WINNING LAND FROM MEXICO

Between 1820 and 1830, many Americans left their homes and wrote the letters GTT on their doors. The letters stood for 'Gone to Texas'. In those years, about 25,000 Americans went to settle in Texas, a territory of Mexico. The Mexican government was giving away land to settlers who would build farms there.

By 1830, the Mexican government was afraid of the Americans in Texas. Many new settlers refused to obey Mexican laws. That year, Mexico stopped allowing Americans into Texas. In October 1835, Texans – led by Samuel Houston – began to fight for Texas's independence from Mexico.

One of the most famous battles was the Battle of the Alamo, a fort in San Antonio. About 200 Texans tried to hold back the Mexican army of 5000 soldiers led by General Antonio Lopéz de Santa Anna. Fighting lasted for 12 days. Fifteen hundred Mexican soldiers were killed. The Texans lost the battle. All the Texas soldiers in the Alamo were killed.

▶ This is a battle scene from the Mexican War in 1846. Most of the battles took place in present-day Mexico, California and Texas. Many Americans and President James Polk wanted to add the region called the Mexican Cession to the United **States**. It included California, Nevada, Utah and parts of Wyoming, New Mexico, Colorado and Arizona.

Texas history
1821 End of Spanish rule. Becomes part of Mexico. Americans begin to settle.
1835 The Texas **Revolution** begins
1836 Texas wins independence from Mexico
1845 Texas becomes the 28th state
1846 War between Mexico and US begins
1848 US gains **territory** called the Mexican Cession
1853 US buys Gadsden Purchase from Mexico.

RED RIVER BASIN 1818
OREGON 1846
LOUISIANA 1803
MEXICAN CESSION 1848
USA 1783
TEXAS 1845
GADSDEN PURCHASE 1853
FLORIDA 1819

◀ This map shows when the United States gained more land from 1783 to 1853.

The Republic of Texas

Samuel Houston gathered more Texas soldiers. On 21 April 1835, they surrounded Santa Anna's troops at San Jacinto, Texas. The Mexicans were quickly crushed and Santa Anna was forced to give Texas its independence. Texas was an independent **nation** for nearly 10 years. It had its own **constitution** and president, Samuel Houston. In 1845, it joined the United States to gain government help.

Another war with Mexico

The United States and Mexico still argued about the Texas **boundary.** In 1846, US president James Polk declared war on Mexico. After nearly two years of battles, the United States won. Mexico sold Utah, California, Nevada and parts of Arizona, New Mexico, Colorado and Wyoming for $15 million. Finally, in 1853, the US bought the Gadsden Purchase from Mexico for $10 million. It included southern Arizona and New Mexico.

◀ This picture of the Battle of the Alamo was painted by Robert Onderdonk in 1905. **Pioneer** Davy Crockett is at the centre of a group of Texans holding back the Mexican soldiers at the Alamo. This building was a Spanish **mission** used as a fort by Texans. On 6 March 1835, the Texans lost the battle. Some historians say Davy Crockett was killed at the Alamo. Others say he was taken as a prisoner and then killed.

AMERICA MOVES WEST

"There is such independence, so much free uncontaminated air. I breathe free without that oppression and uneasiness felt in the gossiping circles of a settled home." Susan Magoffin, a pioneer woman, wrote these words in her diary. Her family was going west in 1846 – like thousands of other Americans.

▼The National Road, the main road west, went from Maryland to Illinois. Here, a stagecoach leaves an inn where passengers, driver and horses have rested.

Filled with hopes and dreams, Americans headed west. They walked, rode horses, sailed boats and rode in wagons. They were called **pioneers** because they were new people coming to a land to claim it for themselves. They came from the eastern **states** in the North and the South. Some crossed the ocean from Europe before joining groups heading west.

Pioneers were usually looking for land to own and farm. Land in the East was expensive, but out West it was cheap. Before the 1840s, most pioneers travelled as far west as Illinois or Missouri. After 1840, they went to Oregon and California.

▼ Heading west, this family loaded their wagon and animals onto a flatboat and travelled down a river.

▲ Along the river banks of Kentucky, Tennessee, Indiana, Illinois and Missouri, pioneers took their flatboats apart and used the wood to build a temporary shelter. Later they would build log cabins.

► ► Pioneers chopped trees and stacked them to make walls for their cabins. Spaces between the logs were filled in with moss, clay or mud. After the roof and fireplace were built, pioneers set split logs into the ground to make a wooden floor.

▲ A religious group, the Mormons, first lived in western New York State. They were always forced to move on by neighbours who did not agree with their beliefs, such as a man having many wives. Their leader, Brigham Young, led them west to the Great Salt Lake in present-day Utah. There, in 1847, they set up a new community.

Working together to get settled

The pioneers usually arrived in the spring, in time to clear the land and plant crops. Neighbours helped each other to clear out rocks, chop trees, move logs and build cabins. A typical log cabin had one room, measuring about 5 by 6 m. Sometimes there was a raised loft for the children's sleeping space.

A family started its new life with perhaps only some kitchen pots and a chair. It built its own tables and benches from logs. It carved its own wooden spoons and bowls and made its own candles and soap. **Pedlars** travelled through new settlements selling some items. As the settlement grew, shops were opened by blacksmiths and other craftworkers.

23

THE ERIE CANAL

Factories sprung up in New York, Massachusetts and Pennsylvania. Cities grew around the factories. By 1825, people were thinking about a better way to transport people and goods. A horse-drawn carriage could move only a small load. A boat in the ocean, on a river or on the Great Lakes could carry much more.

▼ Many **pioneers** started their journey on the Erie Canal. Then they travelled overland, forming a **wagon train** to go west. Meanwhile, in the East the first railroads were being built.

For 100 years, people had talked about building a waterway to connect the Great Lakes to the Atlantic Ocean. In 1812, a man named DeWitt Clinton had a plan to build a canal to do just that. A canal is a waterway dug through the land.

At first, many people laughed at Clinton's idea. They called it 'Clinton's Ditch'. In 1816, Clinton finally received money from the New York state government. A giant eight-year building project began. On 26 October 1825, the Erie Canal opened.

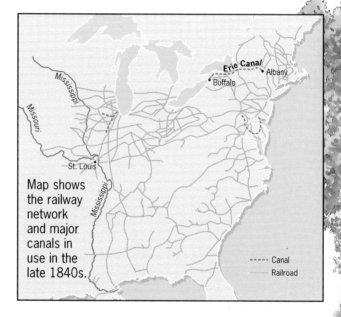

Map shows the railway network and major canals in use in the late 1840s.

Faster and cheaper transport

Hundreds of boats could now travel between Buffalo on Lake Erie to Albany on the Hudson River. Goods were moved by cargo boats. Travellers could pay $1\frac{1}{2}$ cents a mile and ride a slow boat, going 2 miles an hour (3 km/h). Or, they could pay 5 cents a mile and travel at 6 km/h. Either way, canals were better than roads.

Small villages along the 580-km-long canal, such as Utica, Syracuse, Rochester and Buffalo, grew into big towns. New York City on the Hudson River became the country's largest city. When the Erie Canal proved successful, other canals were built in Virginia and Illinois.

▲ Seven million Europeans – mostly from Germany, Scandinavia and Ireland – came to America between 1820 and 1870. Many of these **immigrants** stayed in New York City. Others helped build the Erie Canal or joined wagon trains going west.

◀ Many factories were built in America. By the mid-1800s, coal was the best source of energy for running factory machines. Many people had jobs as coal **miners** in Pennsylvania. This job was dangerous as mine shafts often collapsed.

▲ It took eight years and thousands of workers to build the Erie Canal. With only human and horse power, it was an unbelievably tough job to dig through the hills of New York State, as here at Lockport. The canal was 12 m wide and 1.2 m deep.
  Horses and mules pulled boats through the canal. The animals walked on a path next to the water.

◀ Cutting wood with steam-powered machines first occurred about 1830. Plenty of wood was needed to build canal boats, ocean-going ships for international trade, and warehouses, shops and houses in America's growing cities.

25

MOVING FASTER

Americans were ready for faster transport. People living in the West needed farming supplies from factories in the East. Factories in the East needed cotton from the South and timber and food from the West. Wagons and flatboats were too small and slow. Along came boats and trains that ran on steam power.

In America, in 1807 Robert Fulton invented a steamboat. It could travel at a speed of 8 km/h. Within a few years, Fulton's boats were travelling at 16 km/h. The first steamboats burned wood. Later, they burned coal. By 1860, there were about 1000 steamboats chugging through America's rivers and Great Lakes.

In 1830, Peter Cooper built a steam locomotive that could pull a train at 28 km/h. At first, people were nervous about riding on trains. Would the smoky boiler blow up? Would the speeding train hurtle off the tracks? But by 1850, railways were becoming America's most important form of transport. They could carry large loads over long distances. Trains were travelling almost 50 km/h, while canal boats travelled 6 km/hr.

Railways had other advantages over canals. Railway tracks could be built almost anywhere, not just through flat land. In addition, many canals froze in the winter and could not be used. By 1860, America stopped using canals for mass transport.

▲ America's first steam-powered locomotive arrived from England in May 1829. In Britain, James Watt had invented the steam engine in 1769 and Richard Trevithick developed the first steam locomotive in 1804.

▶ By 1850, New Orleans had become one of America's great ports. Here steamboats on the Mississippi River unload cotton brought from the North. Ocean-going ships transported the cotton to factories on the East Coast of America.

▶ In the mid-1800s, thousands of **slaves** moved from southern **states** to northern states. They were escaping to the North where slavery was against the law. This picture shows slaves on their way to freedom.

In 1850, a law was passed to allow owners to capture slaves in the North and send them back South. People called **abolitionists** helped the runaway slaves. They got many of them to Canada, which was governed by Britain and where slavery was banned. The slaves' secret escape routes and hiding places were called the Underground Railroad.

▲ In 1832, Cyrus McCormick invented a machine called a reaper that helped farmers cut wheat in the fields. This speeded up harvesting. Horses pulled the reaper. McCormick sold his reapers to farmers all over the country.

▲ Steamboats like this one had paddle-wheels powered by steam engines. They could travel up and down rivers. Flatboats could only float in the direction of the river flow. Steamboats carried cargo and passengers.

WEALTH FROM THE SEAS

"The skipper's on the quarter deck, a-squinting at the sails. When up aloft, the lookout sights a school of spouting whales." This was part of the song *'Blow Ye Winds'*. It was sung by whalers who left from small villages on the New England coast of America and sailed the world's oceans in search of great whales.

Whalers had a dangerous job. They might get injured or killed working the sails, or their ship might get destroyed by a whale or wrecked in a storm. Yet it was an exciting and profitable job. By the 1820s, there was great demand for whale oil. Whale oil was made by cutting off the fat under the whale's skin and boiling it. People burned whale oil for light. Fat from one whale could light all the lamps of a small town for many months.

Many whalers lived in seaside villages in Massachusetts and Connecticut. They left their homes and families, sometimes for three or four years, to live aboard whaling ships and sail the oceans. If they were lucky, they would return with many barrels of valuable whale oil and other useful whale parts. The killing, cutting, boiling and packing were all done at sea.

From 1820 to 1850, over 10,000 whales were killed. Whales were in danger of becoming **extinct**. By 1865, the need for whale oil dropped as people began using **paraffin** and then electricity.

▲ Whale oil was burned for light. Whalebone, or baleen, was made into stiffeners for **corsets**. Other whale-parts were made into candles and perfume. The teeth were carved into jewellery.

▼ This picture of 1852 shows a sperm whale destroying a boat. On seeing a whale, the whalers got into smaller boats and rowed closer to throw their **harpoons** at the whale. Since ropes joined the harpoons to the boat, the whale dragged the boat along until it tired out or died in agony.

◀ The best whaling grounds were in the Pacific Ocean. San Francisco was a major whaling port, as in this painting of 1850.

▶ Whalers' wives stood on their balconies to watch for the return of their husbands' ships.

▼ As barrels of whale oil came off the ship, clerks took notes. Other important jobs in a whaling village were:
• timber cutter
• shipbuilder
• barrelmaker
• ropemaker
• sailmaker
• carpenter
• blacksmith
• innkeeper
• shopkeeper.

LIFE ON A WAGON TRAIN

They called it Oregon Fever. Thousands of people packed their belongings in covered wagons and went west. They had heard stories about wheat growing 2 m high and land enough to make everyone rich. The six-month trip took them 3000 km from home, across prairies, deserts and the Rocky Mountains.

A day on the trail
4:00 AM Wake up, eat breakfast, milk cows, take down tents, pack wagons
7:00 AM Hitch the oxen to the wagons and move on along the trail
12:00 noon Stop to eat, rest and feed animals
6:00 PM Stop for the night. Bring the wagons into a circle, make a campfire, cook, eat, sing songs, sleep.

"Those who crossed the plains never forgot the...craving hunger and utter physical exhaustion of the trail, and the rude crosses which marked the last resting places of loved companions. Neither would they ever forget the...sunrise in the mountains; the camp-fire at night...and the pure sweet air of the desert."

A writer named Octavius T. Howe wrote about going west on an 1840s **wagon train**. **Pioneers** needed to travel together. Only the guide in front knew the route. At night the wagons formed a circle to keep out wild animals or attacks from Native Americans who resented the occupation of their lands.

► This engraving of the 1850s by W.H. Cary shows pioneers travelling west.

▼ This is a reconstruction of a trading post at Fort Laramie, Wyoming, where pioneers could buy cooking equipment.

Timing the journey carefully

Before setting out, families met in a 'jumping-off town' such as Independence, Missouri. They started their journey in May, when there was grass along the trail for their animals. If they left too late, they would not make it over the Rocky Mountains by the first snowfall in October.

From 1840 to 1860, over 300,000 people made the journey to Oregon or California. Most pioneers travelled the Oregon Trail. During the summer months, the trail was dry and dusty. Rain turned the trail to mud. Wagon wheels broke. Animals died. Still, the pioneers had to keep on the move. Those that had to cross the Rocky Mountains in the winter usually died.

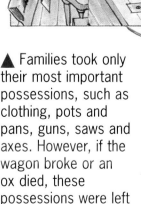
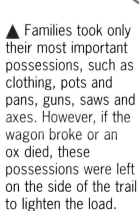

▲ A wagon train was a group of covered wagons that travelled west together. Usually, there were set trails to follow. Small children and their mothers rode in the wagons. So did the injured and sick. Men rode horses. Everyone else walked, keeping an eye on the pioneers' cattle, dogs and chickens.

Wagons were called 'prairie schooners'. From a distance, their white canvas tops looked like sails on a ship. Oxen or mules pulled the wagons. The wagon train travelled 20 to 30 km a day. The trip to Oregon took between 4 and 6 months.

▲ Families took only their most important possessions, such as clothing, pots and pans, guns, saws and axes. However, if the wagon broke or an ox died, these possessions were left on the side of the trail to lighten the load.

▲ All pioneers brought along their cooking utensils. The family chickens laid eggs and the cows provided milk. Men hunted antelope for steaks and prairie-chicken for stews. Pioneers cooked their meals over a camp-fire or under hot coals.

HOUSES IN THE GREAT PLAINS

Great Plains

Many pioneers did not go all the way to Oregon. They made their homes in the Great Plains. This grassy prairie land was good for growing maize, wheat and potatoes, and for raising cattle, pigs and sheep. The Great Plains also had wild thunderstorms, freezing winters, beastly hot summers – and Native Americans.

▲ The Great Plains is a huge area of dry grassland. It is now a major agricultural and mining region.

Pioneers arrived in the **Great Plains** with little money. Most likely, they spent their savings on the wagon and oxen that brought them there, or on rifles and guns to protect themselves from the Native Americans, who had been moved out. Land was cheap, but everything else was very expensive because it had to be transported a long way.

Few trees grew on the plains, so only rich people could afford log cabins. Most people built sod houses, which were made of hard-packed earth and mud. Pioneers cut 'sods' – slabs of grassy earth – and stacked them to make walls. Roofs were also made of earth, laid on top of wooden poles. Grass grew on the roof. Snakes, rats and bugs lived in that grass and they also fell into the house.

Cooking and preserving food

Food was prepared on a cast-iron stove. Corn, or maize, was brought in from the fields and made part of almost every meal. Pioneers ate several kinds of corn bread, such as corn pone, johnnycake and hoecake. They also ate corn on the cob.

Pioneers ate meat, too. Since there were no refrigerators, they found other ways to keep meat from spoiling. They smoked it over a fire, dried it in the sun or soaked it in salty water. Then the meat stayed good for several months.

▶ Sod houses had no running water. A toilet was in a wooden shelter outside the house. It was a simple hole in the ground.

▶ This is an early photograph of pioneers outside their sod house in Nebraska. On a mound above the house, horses pull a wagonload of sods needed to repair the roof. In Britain, the 'cob' houses of Devon, made from lumps of clay, gravel and straw, were built in a similar style.

34

◀ Farmers used a special 'sod-buster' plough to break the tough grass roots. This ox-drawn steel plough was developed by John Deere in 1837.

▼ A family of seven lives in this sod house. The stove in the corner is used for heat and cooking. For fuel, these people burn dried buffalo dung, called 'buffalo chips'. They carry water from a 30-m-deep well they have dug on their farm.

▲ Most pioneers built their own houses, but they often bought the doors and windows by mail order. They picked up their delivery at the nearest **trading post**.

CALIFORNIA GOLD RUSH

In January 1848, John Marshall was working at John Sutter's sawmill near Sacramento, California. He noticed something sparkling beneath his feet. It was gold! Soon the words "Gold at Sutter's Mill!" were being heard around the world.

Merchants' Express Line of Clipper Ships
FOR
SAN FRANCISCO!

NONE BUT A 1 FAST SAILING CLIPPERS LOADED IN THIS LINE.

THE EXTREME CLIPPER SHIP
OCEAN EXPRESS
WATSON, COMMANDER,
AT PIER **9**, EAST RIVER.

This splendid vessel is one of the fastest Clippers afloat, and a great favorite with all shippers. Her commander, Capt. WATSON, was formerly master of the celebrated Clipper "FLYING DRAGON," which made the passage in **97 days**, and of the ship POLYNESIA, which made the passage in **103 days**.

She comes to the berth one third loaded, and has very large engagements.

RANDOLPH M. COOLEY,
118 WATER ST., cor. Wall, Tontine Building.
Agents in San Francisco, DE WITT, KITTLE & Co.

▲ Clipper ships took gold prospectors from New York round South America to San Francisco. This 1851 poster advertises a 100–day voyage on the *Ocean Express*.

On 5 December 1848, President James Polk told **Congress**: "Nearly the whole male population of the country have gone to the gold district. Our commanding officer [fears that] soldiers cannot be kept in the public service without a large increase in pay."

Everyone wanted to get rich quick. People left their jobs and spent their hard-earned savings to travel to California's gold-fields. California's population jumped from 15,000 to 100,000 between 1848 and 1850. At this time, the **nation**'s entire population was 23 million.

▲ When gold nuggets were discovered at John Sutter's sawmill, people swarmed to his land. But he sold off mining rights to prospect for gold too cheaply and, in 1873, he moved to Pennsylvania, bankrupt.

▶ A portrait of George W. Northrup, a gold-miner of 1849.

▼ Gold-miners were also known as prospectors because they were taking a chance and hoping to 'strike it lucky'. They lived in wooden cabins on the gold-fields.

▲ Gold-miners used these tools to pan for gold:
• hammers and pickaxes
• shovels
• water barrels
• bags for gold
• wide metal pans.
The pans were used to swirl around water from the trough, throwing away gravel and leaving the heavy gold at the bottom to pick out.

Mixed fortunes on the gold-fields

The men and women who joined the 1849 Gold Rush were called forty-niners. Some went to California on ships. Most travelled overland, following the Oregon Trail. Many people in Mexico, China, Australia and Europe heard about the Gold Rush. They, too, left home for California to try to get rich.

To find gold, forty-niners first went to a stream and used picks to break up the ground. Next, they shovelled mud and gravel into a wooden trough. Then they poured water from the stream into the trough to wash away everything but the gold. A few lucky forty-niners became rich. Most forty-niners found just a little gold, but had to spend it on food and shelter. Discouraged by the Gold Rush, most of them left the gold-fields and found other jobs in California.

A MINING TOWN

Most miners did not get rich in the Gold Rush. Many shopkeepers did. Miners needed food, clothing, tools and tents. Supplies were low. Demand was high. Many people brought in supplies from the East. They set up a shop and charged sky-high prices. Shoes that cost 75 cents in New York cost $8 in California.

Gold and silver mines were discovered in Oregon, Nevada, Wyoming, Montana, California and Colorado. With each new discovery, people rushed to the site. They left their families at home and promised to come back rich.

Towns sprang up almost overnight. Some miners lived in tents. Others built flimsy shacks. Somebody would open a general store. Another would open a **saloon**. Business would boom. Yet life was far from comfortable. Even water was hard to find. Some people carried it long distances and sold it for lots of money.

▲ The general store sold mining tools, rifles, guns, gunpowder for blasting rock apart, food, clothing and cooking equipment.

▲ In a mining town, houses and shops were built facing each other. The path down the middle was called Main Street. If it looked as if a town would become permanent, the people built sidewalks, or pavements, out of wooden boards.

◀ These miners were photographed in 1852. The men on the left are from European countries. The men on the right are from China.

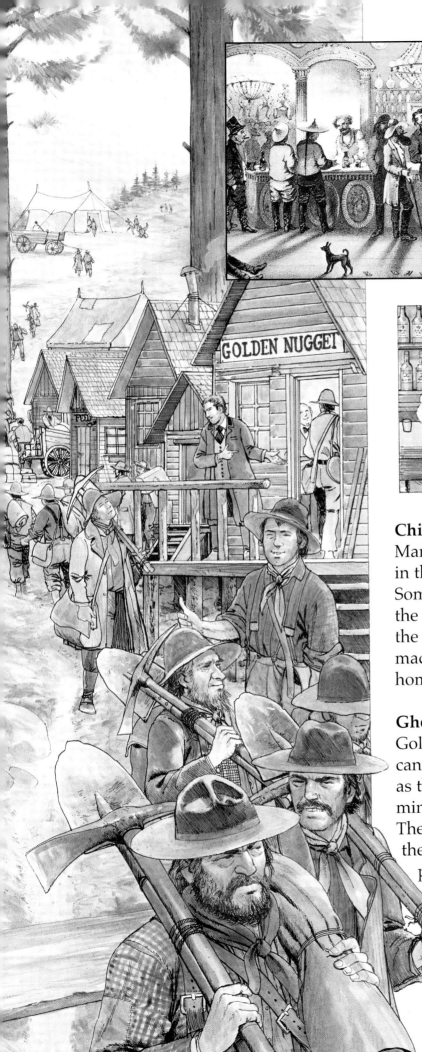

This painting of 1850 shows miners of many nationalities drinking together in a saloon in San Francisco. There were few women in the mining towns because conditions were rough and mining was not considered women's work.

The saloon sold alcoholic drinks such as whiskey, gin, vodka, brandy and beer. After a hard day's work in the mine, miners often spent their evenings – and most of the their money – in the saloon. Often they got drunk and fights broke out.

Chinese immigrants

Many people came from China to work in the mining towns. Most were miners. Some opened businesses. Others became the town's cooks or washed clothing for the townsfolk. Some Chinese people made money in America and returned home. Most stayed in California.

Ghost towns

Gold and silver are natural resources that cannot be renewed as trees can. As soon as the miners found no more metals in a mine, they abandoned it as worthless. There was no reason for them to stay on the land. They moved on to a more profitable location. Some looked for other gold-fields. Most looked for other jobs. Within days, a town could become empty. Then they called it a ghost town.

How many more pegs do we need?

**One flower has four leaves
and the other has three.
How many leaves altogether?**

Pig wants seven apples in his basket.
How many more must he pick?

**Spider has only four shoes.
How many more does he need?**

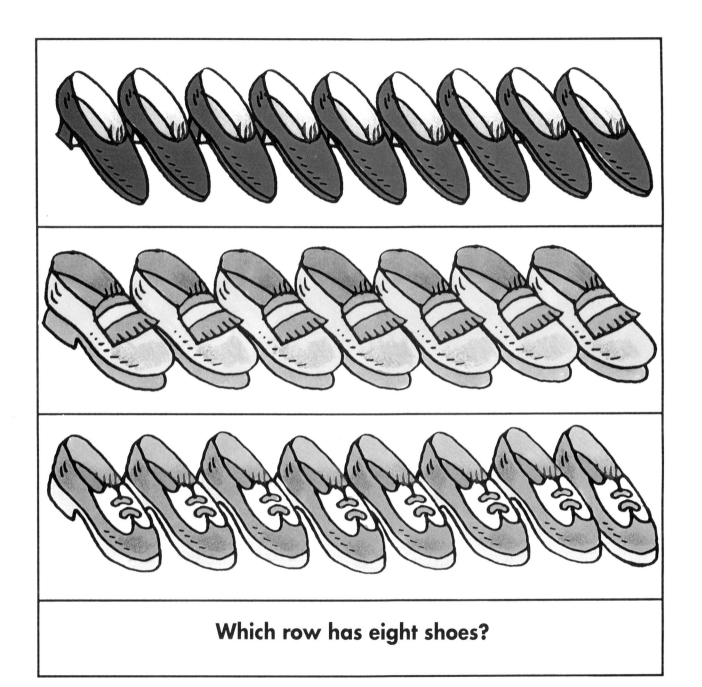

Which row has eight shoes?

Five red balloons and four yellow ones.
How many balloons altogether?

**Mummy hen can see six chicks.
How many more make nine?**

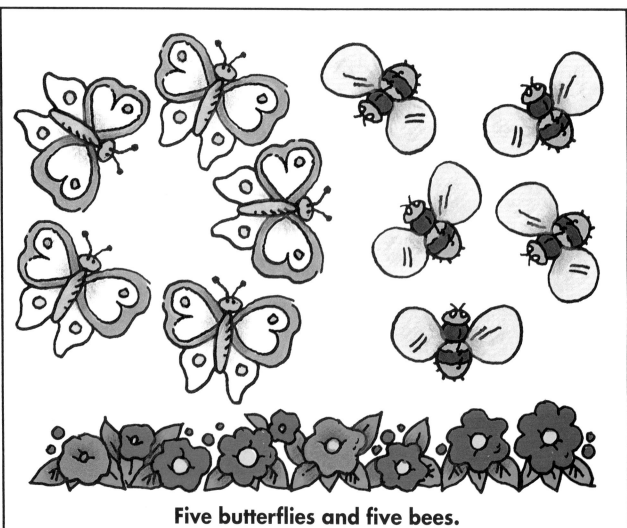

**Five butterflies and five bees.
How many insects altogether?**

$$5 + 5 = 10$$

Ten dolls only have five chairs.
How many more do they need?

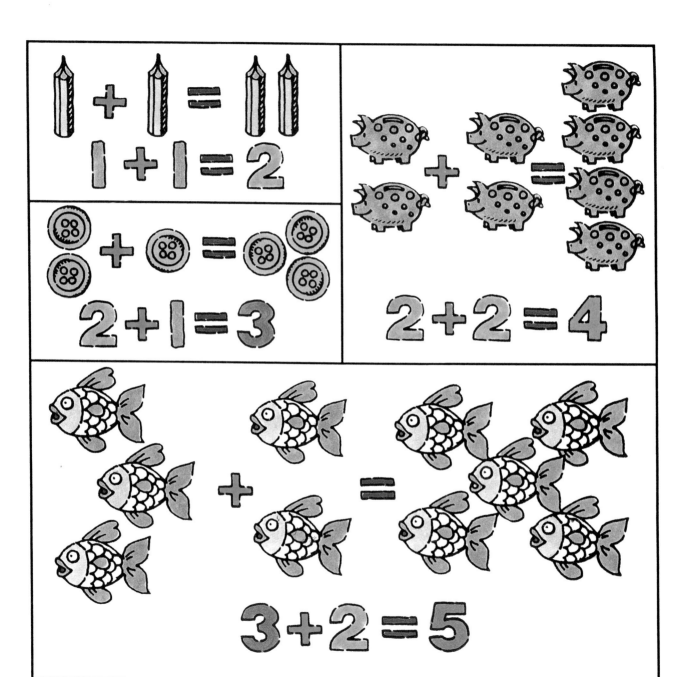

4 + 2 = 6

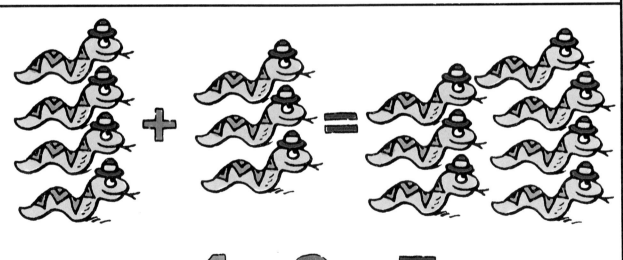

4 + 3 = 7

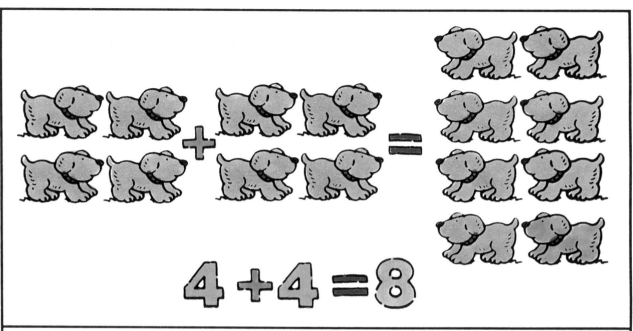

4 + 4 = 8

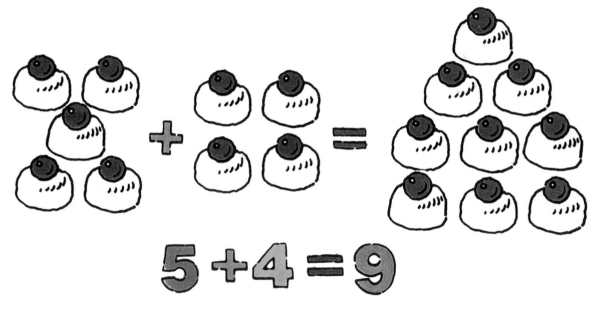

5 + 4 = 9

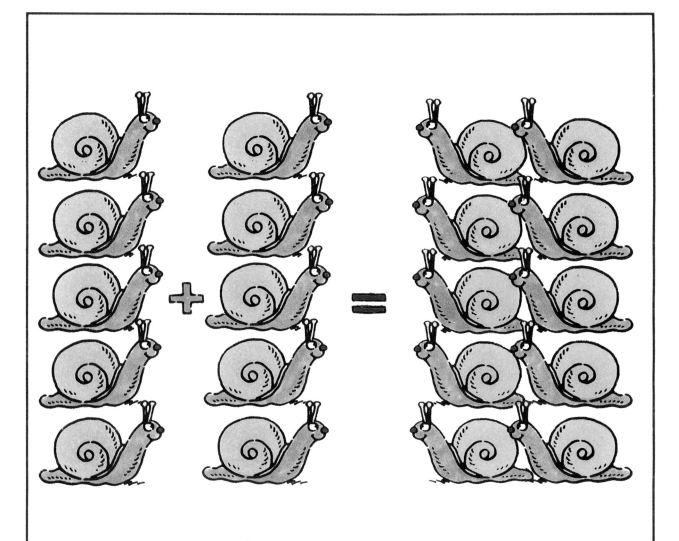

5 + 5 = 10

We hope you
enjoyed learning
about

ADDING

Caroline and John Astrop live by the sea.
They work together on both
illustrations and text for their books.
Surrounded by a large family with children
of all ages, a rich source of ideas and
inspiration, their books are based on the
simple theme that little ones learn more
easily when they are having fun.